Occasional Grace

Also by Deborah Nash Ott:

Twin Soul
a poetry collaboration with Heather Gatley

Paul and Pauline and the Great Pumpkin Flood
a children's book

Occasional Grace

poems

Deborah Nash Ott

GRAYSON BOOKS
West Hartford, Connecticut
graysonbooks.com

GRAYSON
Books

for Jeremy and Jason

Leaf
teach me to fall
on the indifferent earth

—Anna Kamieńska, "Late Summer"

Contents

Ferns

The field guide
is of pocket size
and is brief and simple. —Peterson Field Guide

But ferns are not!
They are Adder-tongue
Limestone
They're Bristle and Brittle
The Bublet Fern will
lead you astray,
So, too the Climbing Fern,
the Filmy Fern.
Fragile Fern
and those Horsetails!
Dwarf!
Kansas!
Marsh!
Slow down, you Rough,
Meadow, Smooth, Swamp,
Variegated Ferns!
I want to find the
Interrupted Fern,
the Lady Fern,
Oh, and dear Merlin's Grass Fern-
cast your spell!
Come, little Polypody,
Speak to me, Quillworts,
Pittered, Riverbank
and Tuckerman's Ferns!
I am running now,
Running Cedar,
Running Moss,
Running Pine,
Enchanted by
Spleenworts, Ebony,

Graves, Green.
And then, oh you
More-than ethereal,
Venus Maidenhead Fern—
I'll find the Water Ferns,
Fruitful,
Leatherleaf
Marginal,
Mountain.
I'll love you all,
Alpine or Blunt-lobed,
Mountain,
Oregon,
Rusty,
Stems underground,
Stalks, fertile.

About Walking in the Woods

It is a natural desire,
to want to wander,
to ponder
that long lost feeling
of being a part of things.
The fungus on the side
of the fallen oak
is a rainbow of mineral shades
with lacy lip like foot of snail.

We look, and soak it in,
learn how to see
the small living world.
Maybe a pine branch muscles its way
through a thicket of bittersweet,
colors dense, the greens,
the ripe red berries, husk of yellow.

It's like human life,
this tumble of brambles and growth,
messy but beautiful.
Souls grow underground,
tree roots converse,
form a quiet network,
and we stop walking,
try to listen.

Seven Instructions from the Book of the World

One:
    Do not start with the sky.
    Begin with the ceiling of your room,
    empty and bland,
    a canvas of plaster and paint,
    a whiteness,
    a tabula rasa.

Two:
    Go outside.
    Grab a clod of dirt
    in your hungry hands,
    mix it with a dabble of water
    from a small puddle,
    appreciate that minerals and mud
    provide something satisfying,
    slippery and primal.

Three:
    Get to know your rocks.
    Some are glum and noncommittal,
    but you'll find a few.
    sacred and powerful,
    glittering mica, basalt,
    recognize them,
    one or two might befriend you—
    consider yourself favored.

Four:
    Get lost in the forest.
    A young pine
    could point the way to safety,
    trust an old oak,
    or make peace with the wildflowers,

you know, the ones you plucked as a child,
the ones that should stay put.
They're ready to forgive you—
Columbine, for instance, has a big heart.

Five:
Choose the ocean,
the lake, the river,
the element that buoys you,
carries your stories in waves,
tides, thundering falls.
Make sure you understand water,
and even if you think you do,
dive in again,
you're just skimming the surface.

Six:
Can we skip mankind for now?
Let's just move onto fauna—
you know what you're drawn to,
a deer, a dolphin, a dragonfly,
a stallion, carry you away,
study the integrity of the dung beetle.
Are we ready to sideline our worries,
to embrace those of a bird
on the wing before a storm?

Seven:
And, speaking of birds,
now you can look to the sky,
impossible blue,
turbulent gray, chilling white,
or a hot, dissolving red.
Reach up to that
source of light,
because where else will you find

the quiet, insistent rules
that make you revel in the day,
bow to the night?

Find a kinship in the moon and the planets
    and those raggedy stars,
    the ones you wanted to paint on your ceiling,
    the ones that will guide you
    so much better
    out into the night.

You will be gazing, breathless.

Future

I fetched the paper this morning.
Through the tall pines, in the haze
a less-than-full moon, still white
just on the wane, invited me to linger.
I stood on the driveway and breathed in,
the pines and the moon,
the six AM promise,
and everything being rewritten.

Eight Sacred Horses

If one could thank an emperor,
one might give a nod to King Mu,
who conceived of eight sacred horses.
I have a set, a reproduction of a dream,

that I played with as a child, unbroken.
They lift me now from my weighted days, these
tiny, porcelain, white, wild little things
which should be in a museum, or painted

on a generous vase, breathing life
into each maned, magical beast
Every one a power, a presence,
numbered, by that Chou leader, the least

of which is Number One, who gallops
with swift hooves, so fast
that no contact takes place
with the dusty road, no load

slows the mare, no other power unnerves
her, least of all Horse Two, who runs
faster than the winged birds,
as if to take flight but, carrying our emperor

who will admire as much his Number Three,
a steed of night, racing
in darkness, covered, perhaps by a
velvet shroud, obscuring his pale glow,

as horse Number Four runs with sun and shadow
off on a chase, o precious mare,
who pairs herself with the burning orb,
in the shade, silent, pursuing night,

heedless of Number Five, a beauty
of silken mane and coat and tail, forcing poets'
hands to write of the ephemeral,
the painful perfection of what is unattainable,

she, too, moves with Number Six, but falls
behind as he is a blur, ten replicas of his
presence racing, crashing into the future
of place, and of meeting one's image along the way,

and Number Seven, who floats above, upon a cloud,
powers allowed her to shift her shape
on mist and wispy flowering billows,
King Mu, you would rise on high with her

to meet with Number Eight, who has wings,
a Pegasus of the East, carrying you, and anyone
who dared to travel with equine dreams, gallop
or run or otherwise escape this heavy, ponderous world.

What Sedona Had to Offer

The sun, yes, and the brittle running fence,
a hummingbird busy flower-busting
insolent cacti, an amber dragonfly.

And Magis, the blue-black stallion,
seventeen hands high,
cold fire and delight,
a force, with constant, watchful eye
a healing horse, a spirit, a god.

The drum circle in the teepee
did not interest him;
the carrot I brought him each morning did.

Soft muzzle, velvet lips,
reaching out like a separate being
apart from head or eye or ear.
He waited and watched,
cool desert blanket,
corral not yet dusty.

When he escaped
I grabbed the bait,
to coax the giant home.
But deep inside my equine heart
I rode him bareback,
into the rough and heedless desert,
untethered and alone.

Seasonal Report

August
    Left too long in the sun,
    summer glow burns to an angry red,
    tender evenings ignored,
    waters lapping,
    never sought.
    Tufts of grass
    parched, dry as ash.

October
    Fruit burgeoning, the Rome Reds
    dropped unnoticed, ripened,
    softened, then shriveled,
    turned brown,
    harvest lost.
    Two or three saved—
    they were the sweetest.

December
    Who failed to bring in
    the tiny maple sapling
    from the first snow?
    Frozen ground, frozen roots
    cannot thaw without damage.
    Winter mornings, the ice sheen
    of Nod Brook is passive gray,
    reflecting only sky.

April
    Cruel times come with bulbs bursting.
    A robin returns too early,
    carcass mixed with gray slush
    of the last spring storm.
    A time of old beginnings,

of tired resurrections,
and judgment hangs
like droplets in the air:

It could have been a better year.

On Mingo Beach

You lived not far from here once,
you might have waded these waters,
cold Atlantic inlet,
on a sparkling summer day
and here, I pause and lean against
the lichen-covered boulders;
they are like temple gods,
witness to all passings.

You passed, my friend,
and I wander, now,
the ebbing tide, the waves
draw from my feet,
like fingers pulling away;
it is your reach, gently receding.

I spy two women
who swim together—
earlier, they'd walked me here;
I'd lost my way.
a kindness given freely,
not unlike all the acts of kindness
you'd done for me.

I reach for a clam shell,
smooth, white interior,
seaweed encrusted on top;
with a little scrubbing
it would make a lovely bowl,
then I think better
and replace it on the sand.

Let those things be in nature,
let the heart grieve untouched;

there is goodness for all of us
on Mingo Beach.

The Towpath

A canal of this reach
deserves a theater of names,
"the Erie" seems too short
for this wide ribbon of water,
over 300 miles long
carved by pickax, shovel.

Men moved mud and rocks
the ribbon filled, linked
the Hudson with one Great Lake,
crisscrossed the Mohawk—
constructed aqueducts,
marvelous madness for amateur builders,
new to a forested land.

Birchbark canoes carried animal furs,
timber, then the bateaux were brought in,
heavy boats, loaded, three feet deep,
pulled along the newly-beaten path
by mules, hot and dusty.

This animal power, harnessed
slow and steady on a hot August day,
upstate New York, a land
just south of Ontario.
Canada geese slapped their wings
against the green-brown flow,
announced their presence and the
creation stories, silent below.

What workers made this?
Who paid the final price?
Not just the diggers
but the mothers and wives,

the children, who barely recognized
their fathers the color of soil.

Taverns and guest houses
absorbed the night men
and their rough ways
vulgar, perhaps, after long days,
laborers of a liquid frontier.
This canal could not have been
without the labor of 50,000 men.

One thousand died in its making,
in toil and fatigue, in accidents
battling earth and stone.

The Finger Lakes

My nephew waded out to his waist
in Canandaigua Lake. He was a solid young man,
but his mother warned him.

Though she was unaware of the drop-off
from waist-high to 276 feet,
I said nothing, but watched him swim.

A few strokes and he was in the depths
while she fretted from the shore.
I was confident, he was vital and strong,

buoyed by his youth
and good conditioning. He swam with grace
and I turned to the mother, smiled.

He's 29; he's an athlete, the darkness
will not reach him; there are no surprises
at that age, none except the chance meeting of a love.

I nodded my head to the August sky.
He'll do just fine, I told her; it's not so deep.
And yet, I knew about the cold hand of still water.

He will return, no doubt. But that I longed
to swim out further and dive below,
she had no idea. He would resurface, not I.

Scrambling

It was the hardest part of the climb,
shale spilling down the mountain,
grey and glistening,
slippery even, lined
by scrub pines and Alpen rose,
the rare Edelweiss.

But the silt rock waited
and we had no choice,
lean in, angle the legs,
imitate the mountain goats
gazing at us from on top
like white, horned gods,
feigning boredom,
with their strange goat eyes,
chewing dew-covered grass.

We walked on shards as slick as oil,
the loose river which divides safe
from dead, a fall from the solid earth
to unforgiving chasm.

He first. Then me,
laughing a little.

Bumper Stickers

Say a man gives you the finger at a stop light
and you decide to smile in return.

And then you both pull into the same gas station,
he, unaware that your eyes are drilling his back.

And let's assume he buys one of those hot dogs
that rotate on oily rods all day, overcooked

like the look he gives when you pass him in the doorway—
he sees that it's you, the one he saluted in the car.

And you've purchased, let's say, a ten-dollar scratch card,
on a whim, a hope, a desperate plunge into chance

like the risk you took in greeting the stranger's gesture
with the opposite of whatever dark impulse brought his middle digit

into your view, you, who proudly sport bumper stickers
that say My Body My Choice, and Love is Love

is what angered the man, who is now looking at you
as you rub away numbers to reveal a losing card.

He's sizing you up, you're white and female,
maybe a veil of regret passes over his face, and he says

Hey I hope you've got a winner there,
and you, let's assume, have had enough of this,

think, you're glad you resisted temptation,
bit your tongue before telling the guy to fuck off.

And then you both pull away, you, content, perhaps,
that when he went low you went a little higher,

but hoped that the hot dog rebelled in his stomach,
and you felt somewhat witch-like, your talismans

being the urgent messages on the rear of your car,
words that provoke, words that rattle.

After the Shooting

Buffalo, New York

He described stepping over bodies
as he was led from the freezer,
what they wore, the colored clothing,
the strides he'd managed, careful
not to trample a finger.
He was cold and his eyes were downcast,
mind riddled by the muffled shots—
he was stuck in the cooler.

She listened, later,
an inherited chill,
the splay of a Jim's Ribs t-shirt,
the tie-die yoga pants,
witnessed all with him,
stomach coiled and ready to spring.

I can never unsee that, he said.
I can never unhear that, she thought.

Sashiko

a form of functional embroidery that originated in Japan.

Hearts worn by sorrow also need mending,
the needle will pierce the cloth of pain,
the life we know is always upending
and must be healed, though scars will remain.

Repairs of this kind demand real trust
in one who can fix with deft, gentle hands,
an organ so vital, so precious, which must
heed the soul's tender commands.

That to be human is to be open to hurt,
to care for another can lead to an ache
of such magnitude that only time will convert
from sadness to love for love's sake.

Keep nimble with fingers ready to sew
together a threadbare life, then let go.

Labyrinthine

Two people emerge from her office,
man and woman, not a couple,
more like brother and sister,
or charge and caretaker,
and they get lost in the halls,
turning this way and that,
the hatted, overalled younger brother,
the matronly, rain-coated sister.

This is what I pretend,
as they wander, searching for the exit,
talking softly to one another,
patient, serious, they find the door,
the stairs, descend.

I want to guide them,
help them find the right way,
but who am I to lead?
And maybe they need
that time to wander,
to decompress before they go.
It is, after all, cruel out there
in the suburban world.
One has to be ready
for the daily onslaught.

And so, instead, I wait to be summoned,
to get lost in my own maze.
My GPS is on high alert,
and the tracking data
is almost too much.
It is memory, it is regret,
it is the fragile hope
of second chances.

Tightrope

With the ones we love
we are always on the line,
seeking balance.

In the leveled darkness,
during those furrowed days,
there might be blood,
there is certainly pain.

We'll hold fast just so long,
mouths open,
amazed that our hearts
can sustain the weight,
that our animal feet can grip at all
on a weathered rope,
eyes on our own souls, and theirs.

We are bound from ship to shore
but our focus will surely come undone.
The cord is taut, yet we, unsteady,
cannot find equilibrium.

Teaching Tragedy in High School

The room is clammy, air conditioned,
windowless,
public education, Connecticut style—
The text: a tragedy
The topic: dramatic structure

On the whiteboard, I draw a pyramid,
exposition, rising action,
climax (some tittering),
falling action, resolution.

Students stare,
the visual perk lasts a few seconds,
my question posed:
Where in the play
is the turning point,
that moment
of highest intensity?

One hand raises,
the owner a tattooed,
nose-ringed, black-eyed beauty:
Would it be, he takes the poison?

Others?

She stabs herself!

I pause.

Wheel it back, what action
defined the tragic downfall?
What called the shots on all the rest?

Silence sucks energy
out of the space,
a boy checks his phone,
and then nose-ring
makes another attempt:

It was the fact that they were born at all,
it's all so fucking hopeless.

I ignore the language,
have kids move desks
to form a circle, look at each other,
and finally, finally we talk about life,
and what the Hell happened
to happy endings.

Construction Site

For months that suburban street
lay unfinished; often
we would wander from the bare
newness of her parent's split level
and stop where the asphalt did,
at a dusty trench of cement sacks,
hardened like bricks, discarded lumber
cut at odd angles, a Coke bottle,
remnants of men working—
nearby, an airy frame, roofless.

We'd stare at this world's end,
be a little afraid, and in silence
retreat to Nancy's house,
relieved that neither of us
dared the other to explore further.

We'd heard about dark
things in empty lots,
on the edge of the tract.

And when I dream of this,
I am in agony, caught
like a figure on a book jacket,
forever walking toward
something unfinished,
the smell of tar and sawdust
dizzying me, and my friend
has turned away,
left me to wander in this
childhood fear. I am scared
to step over the builder's trash,
I might stumble, cut myself,
I might bleed.

Ground Sparrows

My childhood friend, Nancy, and I
discovered a nest at the base of a tree

Three hatched chicks, bellies distended and pink,
mouths silent and open, eyes shiny black.

And we touched each one, tentative, gently
entranced by their frailty as well as their energy.

Later we visited the nest again
to find the three chicks all slain.

We told my father in somber tones
and he shook his head wisely, *You invaded their home.*

Your smell (our smell!). We had touched new life;
the mother had pecked them and left them to die.

We'd tainted a place where mystery lies,
 avoided that tree, and each other's eyes.

Making Oatmeal

There is hope in this act,
and a little reverence.

The meal will nourish
and there will be more cold mornings,

steel cut oats, sweet maple syrup,
the grinding plows on the street below.

When I was young, I wrote a poem
about an old man raking leaves

with the vim and vigor of a teenager;
I admired him deeply.

And now I think I was courting hope
even then, in my solitary, big-house

one-parent-just-moved-out days,
a New York autumn settling in.

What matters then, is the act
of cooking, writing, watching,

of risking each new breath.
I will plan for more small repasts,

wind through the seasons well,
nodding to the dark days,

holding the favor of this life,
gratefully, like a warm bowl in my hands.

In Media Res

When he emerged from the water,
after the cannonball dare,
after the gathered friends
with cocktails and canapes
laughed at his antics,
when that part of the show was over,
he smiled, black hair glistening,
climbed from the pool,
and his wife smiled too.
But she was still inside his cannonball,
crashing in the chlorinated waste,
no chance of breathing,
immersed, the awkward plunge,
the sweet bathing costume, floating.
And she wondered what it would feel like
to be the life of the party.

Why Mother Had Him Leave

It was not his drinking,
never the port wine bottle
half empty on the counter,
nor his big laughing belly,
and he never laid a hand on her,
just drank, and smoked his Pall Malls,
after a day of engineering.

It wasn't the camping trips,
though I'm sure she hated them,
barely tolerated the canvas tent.
It wasn't even his crude humor,
the vulgar joke; Mother would feign disgust,
then titter in that adult way,
a young girl could hear all of this.

It was about, she said,
his silences, a brooding sort,
a missing connection,
a head shaking no, no, no.

They fought: who would go?
Who would stay?
He moved upstairs,
to the finished attic,
and then he moved away.

Light Baggage

I remember the train tickets to Milan,
the shiny hotel pamphlets,

my mother's Burberry coat,
my sons' two backpacks.

Italian lira and passports,
a camera with fresh film,

stamped passes to the cathedral roof
where I snapped a photo of her at the top.

Impossible blue of the northern Italian sky,
glowing sun, menacing gargoyles,

and Mother, stepping along the narrow walkway,
smiling, then laughing, marveling at the view,

marveling that an Indiana girl, born in the Depression
could be at these heights on this day, in Italy.

We descend again, bags of dried corn given as prizes—
my boys feed the fluttering pigeons,

where there is happiness on the Piazza del Duomo,
Heaven, later, at the Terra Gelato,

and my mother saying *I cannot believe I am here,*
I cannot believe what I'm seeing.

First Snow and Darkness

It takes its time to descend,
but then the effect is irreversible
Cluster of pines, needles lacy white
hold the snow willingly.
The great freeze is here, flakes
silent in the dark afternoon.
And not unlike winter's descent,
an aging mother might feel as though
she is falling, like dust, in a flurry
of quiet care, in a small room
of a nursing home, lacy curtains
at the window, on the table
a stuffed bear, a potted mum
from Thanksgiving
holding its amber-gold, remarkable,
so that the daughter comments,
as she always did,
how bright and fine this place is,
how warm and welcoming,
the squall waiting outside.

I Dreamt My Mother Went to Mars

I dreamt my mother went to Mars
and returned with stories of survival where
she thrived amongst the rocks and dust
and breathed the thin atmosphere.

She said she'd take me back next time
on some cataclysmic day
when Earth was simply too much
for women like us to stay.

As on that planet, cold and grim
there was a sense, (or so she said)
that in this desert-like world, peace lived.
Breathe lightly, let it go to your head.

A planet for women, cold and bare
and totally devoid of men—
we'd raise our children quietly there,
a chance for us to begin again.

The Martian Sun, the Martian wind,
we'd make a government of joy,
we'd build our sub-terranean town
and teach every girl and boy

to value each strange shard of light,
to handle all with love and care,
to grow our hydroponic plants,
to celebrate the harvest there.

Every boy would be wise and free
and every girl incredibly strong.
We'd raise our voices to the galaxy
in our space suits, and chant a song

to Phobos and Deimos, the two moons,
and to all that is fair and all that is good.
A cold and lonely planet no more,
we'd stand where no man had stood.

A mother's dream becomes the daughter's,
this daring new world, this life on Mars.

At 68

Each October I must clear the garden,
the lower one that no one sees from the street,
but I enjoy it from below, inside or outside,
Hosta and bee balm, black-eyed Susans
all at eye level—the garden is raised,
the basement, subterranean.

At no one's invitation, I clip and clear,
apologize to the black beetle or sleepy bee,
the ones that thought they'd found a place
to curl into, to draw nourishment from, to hide.
It is quiet work; my mind softens in the autumn light.

And I think of my mother who never did this,
never cleared her garden when she was my age—
she had none, rented an apartment
years after leaving my father, lived alone,
surrounded by prints of Renoir and Rembrandt,
a Van Gogh perhaps, with no blooms
to trim, no bins to fill; just frames to dust.

And yet, she might have enjoyed this,
like a child embracing a chore for the first time,
hanging the laundry, perhaps,
the fresh sheets snapping, the delight
in doing a task, yes, she would have gleaned
some satisfaction, the novelty of it all,
beds ready for winter, brown mulch, waiting,
bulbs quiet in the pre-winter soil.

Inheritance

My mother hoarded dolls,
hundreds of them, peach-ruffled ones,
Alpen children with tiny rucksacks,
a bejeweled princess, a Grace Kelly,
Betsy McCalls, dozens of Barbies,
a couple of Kens and G.I. Joes,
an Asian gem, porcelain face,
jet-black hair, red silk kimono.
Dolls, all,
and they haunt me now,
the precious and the rare,
left to me when Mother passed.
And I sold them, arranged them
in my musty garage, parting ways
and handing them over
to grateful buyers,
those sparkling model dolls,
soft pink baby dolls
with kits of clothing,
laundered and ironed.
Some untouched, never-displayed,
fresh in their boxes, Flapper dolls
wrapped in boas and pearl strings
svelte gowns of black velvet—
they stared at me in the darkness
on sale day, some with accusatory eyes,
asking why would I part with them—they were so loved.
All stole my mother's heart,
all fulfilled the promise
of eternal youth and beauty,
unlike me, the mediocre daughter,
unlike me, who could not compete.

Smoke Rises

Smoke rises from the house behind my own,
we share the same lot, same trees,
a wandering creek.

We have heard one another
of a summer night perhaps,
a sneeze, a shout, a loud TV,

But never have we spoken, oh perhaps
a nod exchanged on walks around
the oval loop when I admire their grounds,

see, on winter days, my own house
through the bare trees, its back,
with looming, empty windows.

I wonder if they wonder who I am,
what shared delights we have
in our separate lives.

Two houses, divided by water and land,
and when I leave or die,
we'll have never even shaken hands,

though we breathed the same air,
trod the same pavement,
gazed at the same sky.

Prism

This is city life at its quietest.
My partner and I move through darkened halls,
preparing for a dim night's journey,
the hissing of tires on wet pavement
lulls us to sleep. We are drifting

with the faint siren that flows through our dreams,
with the death the vehicle may bring us.
Then, all is in a silent hold, in a looming house,
breathing noiselessly.

The chipped gray paint, the warped boards
signal a muted plea. This place is old and dust-laden.
We may shine each piece of stained glass
in the morning. Meanwhile,
the glass is what colors our dreams;
moonlight seeps through and prisms the walls.

Glad for the sunrise, we
corner taunting fears for another day,
baby the kitten, toy with the idea of a new life
envision poppies in a lush garden,
well-planned it would be—
the time will come.

This is our condition. Cultivated,
it enhances us, but when another evening creeps
along on a winter's eve,
we may think to ask that old question, *Why?*
or move the potted fern
closer to the window,
where it can catch more light.

Occasional Grace

I have a diagnosis
that I rarely talk about.

It is a boogeyman, or woman,
or some gender-free disease
that fills my blood with too much white.

Those relentless, ghost-like
cells will duplicate, damaged,
imperfect. I'd rather not say
what they're up to.

Better to embrace the cold January sky,
blue and beckoning,
accept the invitation
of a few muscular clouds
that call out—

C'mon, it's winter,
you can do this,
sing in the morning,
walk at noon.
Stay on the trail
and don't turn around.
Your numbers haven't
hit the ceiling,
not yet.

Not with snow falling just now,
covering, with grace,
the leaf-littered path.

Iceberg

A23-a, the size of three Manhattans, in Antarctica

You're liberated now,
unstuck from the Filchner ice shelf
to which you were
so coldly attached,
and ungrounded from the floor
of Wendell Sea.
You float now, freely,
pirouetting your way around,
a 40 mile turnstile of flat white,
like God's handkerchief,
pristine,
and heading towards your doom.
Doom!
You've left the mother ice,
and head north
where the sad process will begin,
the melt, the slow, steady disappearance
in a vast Southern ocean,
in time, reduced to the size of a life raft.
You behave like a memory,
one that shaped your past,
but is now adrift,
until you give way,
deepen your salty host
and vanish
in the level rising.

The Hours

The day is anxious,
taking aim at
the young couple
who just moved in.

I've heard them upstairs—
the laughter, some lovemaking,
and then quiet.

Now, she ignites the new day,
her red orange locks
tangled in scarf and wind,
a target in the parking lot.

I watch her, done up in
boots and flannel,
her partner following,
unsure, hair tousled.

The car turns, grinds,
it is cold and he cannot start it,
and then he can.

From my window,
I quietly wonder
how we yield, again and again
to that mystery
which our eyes open to
each morning,
and how these youth,
live in that eternal question:
Why are we here?

Of an aging Ulysses, Tennyson once wrote
that much is taken,
though much abides.
These two pilgrims
embark on a long journey
and I wish them well,
even as they turn into the rush of traffic,
even as the hours take them in.

Two Men at a Literary Festival

One is tweed-capped
and corduroyed,

the second, all in black,
is tired, rests his head

on the other's shoulder—
they have visited many booths.

Earlier their quiet talk
was focused on a shiny book.

The dark one paid for the copy,
then began to cry,

told his friend he had to sit
and, after some silence, said

She knew everybody,
she knew their worth.

Eavesdropping at the Big Y

I was in the international aisle
searching for salsa.
They were on their knees,
stocking shelves with frijoles,
rows of them. *I'm so hurt*
one of them said.
I can't move forward,
I keep thinking about her,
about what she did,
about how she left me.
I just can't go on.
He stood and turned away.
The other one remained
kneeling, nodding,
a can of enchilada sauce
in one hand,
stilled for that moment.
Hey man, he said
You need to talk more?
We could go out for a meal
or fix dinner together
or whatever—
you don't have to do this alone.
And I listened, amazed,
wanted to thank them
that I was witness to
this moment.
These men,
under the indifferent neon light
of a grocery store,
offering up to each other
what neither would
win or fight over.

Life Cycle of the Luna Moth

Black egg clings, grows mouth,
eats the tender leaf, hungry
small, mighty monster

Pupa hope glistens
life within, slow unfolding
metamorphosis

Now she does not eat
simply recalls the sumac
sweet gum, persimmon

Silent light draws her
she is of the night, she flies
unseen, moon-bidden

Luna needs more time
these thirty days
cruel, this cycle

Silk, sea-green goddess
lifeless on the hot pavement
lovers pause, sidestep

It's never enough
to just be the moth, she must
die with ragged wings

Emily Dickinson Meets John Lennon

Imagine it takes place
somewhere like Heaven.

Two minds, quiet in kind
the buzzing flies have stilled.

The slant of light, a single blind
these citizens of the world.

Untethered by possession
or fealty, no heaves of civil storm.

But the Peace of the bee
hovering over flower cup.

The carriage bringing the two
home to another country,

John, she will say, *you have
a soul as present as the sky.*

And Emily, John would say,
you are the wind I cannot feel,

*The empty space of surrender
when a dreamer gives up the dream*

Whether or Not

Whether or not they exist, we're slaves to the gods.
—Soares, The Book of Disquiet

And so we think again
that the sky is full of our fate.

Cool powers look down, laugh
shake their heads.

Poor humans, so blind,
most of us, to the gem

of life right before our eyes,
the miracle of the uterus,

the curling leaf, the kitten's fur,
nothing we can truly comprehend.

Beginnings and endings abound,
the bleached coral, the melting ice,

the victims of our carelessness
homeless, scorched, or washed away.

It is the cat o' nine tails,
handed to us by those unfeeling gods,

and we'll say we deserved it,
or we'll say nothing at all.

Acknowledgments

Grateful acknowledgment is made to the editors of the following publication where these poems first appeared:

Connecticut Bards Poetry Review 2025 (Local Gems Press): "The Hours"

Connecticut Bards Poetry Review 2022 (Local Gems Press): "Tightrope"

My deep gratitude goes to the first reader of this collection, Heather Gatley for her valuable feedback and belief in the merit of this collection. Additional thanks go to the Farmington Valley Chapter of the Connecticut Poetry Society, whose members provided critiques in a spirit of friendship and comradery. I am also grateful for the encouragement and guidance from The Magic Theatre Poetry Reading group, the Four Ladies, and Brittany Mihalich.

Finally, heartfelt thanks to Ginny Lowe Connors for her generous support and wisdom, and for the attentive care with which she edited this collection.

About the Author

Deborah Nash Ott is originally from Rochester, New York but she lived and worked abroad for many years. Her short stories and poems have been published in small presses in the United States and Switzerland. Several of her memoirs have appeared in www.memoirist.org. Her novella, *The Canopy*, was selected for the Farmington Libraries Connecticut Indie Book Project. She also co-published *Twin Soul*, a collection of poems she wrote with Welsh poet Heather Gatley. Additionally, her work has appeared in *The Connecticut Bards Poetry Review*. Deborah loves the writing life and deeply values the connections she has made with fellow poets. She lives and writes in West Hartford, Connecticut.